EXCHANGE EMOTIONAL PAIN FOR PEACE AND PROSPERITY

Cheryl T. Long

Ordering Information:

Quantity sales. Special discounts are available on quantity purchases by corporations, associations, and others. For details, contact me at

www.deardaughterslovesmom.com

Printed in the United States of America

Dedication

This book is dedicated to "Self-Love" because "Self-Love" is the greatest love of all!!!

Acknowledgments

First and foremost, I would like to thank God. In the course of putting this book together, I appreciated how true this gift of writing is for me. You've given me the power to believe in my passion and follow my dreams. I could never have done this without the faith I have in you, the Almighty.

To my Mom and Dad Elizabeth and Kenneth: "For the first time in 40 years, I am speechless! I can barely find the words to express all the wisdom, love, and support you've given me. You are my #1 fans, and for that, I am eternally grateful."

To my children, Devon, Anjanae, Shinera, and Robyn: "You are the best thing that I have ever done in my life! You welcomed me into motherhood, and I am so grateful for all of you. Mommy loves you more than you will ever know, and know this my writing is proof of the beauty I see whenever I look into your eyes!"

Table of Contents

Introduction... 1

Chapter 1 5

How to Leverage Your Emotional Pain for
Peace and Prosperity 5

Chapter 2 15

How to Live in Peace Despite Suffering in
The World 15

Chapter 3 19

How to Stop Living in the Hurt.................... 19

Chapter 4 25

How to Relieve the Feeling of Emptiness . 25

Chapter 5 32

HowTo Relieve the Feeling of Emptiness as
a way to peace and prosperity.................. 32

Chapter 6 47

How to Overcome Grief and Pain 47

Chapter 7 63

How Meditation Can Help You 63

Chapter 8 67

Think Healthy, Be Healthy......................... 67

Conclusion 74

About Author.. 75

More Books by the Author...................... 76

Introduction

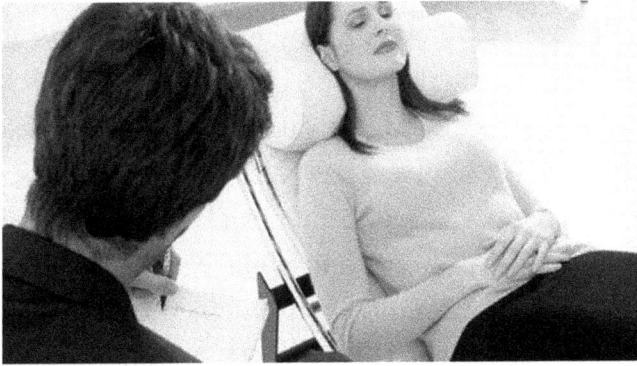

It seems to me that, in our journey of living with pain, one of the central ingredients which is really helpful is to cooperate with pain; to allow what is showing up here and now in your life to have the space to be there. Just this attitude has a transformative effect and impact. When we agree with what life has brought this day and this very moment, our relationship to it changes — it transforms. It sounds basic to allow things to be as they are, to go with the flow.

Many people use this "go with the flow" in a cliched way. For most people who live with chronic pain, telling them to go with the flow will often provoke a response like; "well to put it mildly, you have no idea what it's like to live with this pain. If you were in my shoes, I don't think you would be advising me to go with the flow!"

Those of you who live with serious chronic pain will know exactly what I mean. When other well meaning people advise you about how to deal with pain but obviously have ZERO personal experience of it, it just doesn't work. They just actually don't understand what it's like. For some time now, I've learned and accepted that their well intentioned advice is just that — A well intentioned advice.

The fact still remains, but there is a way to go with the flow of pain. That is by allowing what shows up today to be there: to have the space and a place in your life. Accept what comes today. When pain shows up, understand that life has brought it: life is showing up as pain. It seems pretty obvious that pain often shows up as a warning that something is wrong and that thing needs to be attended to and fixed. Nobody likes being in physical pain, and everyone has the right to live a pain-free life.

However, what happens to those of us on whom nothing works? No matter what medicine, alternative therapies, or whatever healing modalities we try, nothing seems to work. What then?

In my experience, this is where we need to turn to a dimension of life beyond our normal day-to-day experience. This dimension is often accessed by prayer, meditation, submission, or by simply giving up and giving over to a presence, an energy, God, a Being, Christ, Tao, or Allah. Whatever name you give it — that is deeper, vaster, stronger, more intelligent and loving than the very pain you experience in your body — is fine.

Turning towards the pain, accepting it, allowing it, and even welcoming it with a submissive orientation to this deeper dimension of ourselves,God and Being, is the only consistent way I have discovered to live in freedom with pain. It's like some sort of miracle happens. The presence meets the pain and transforms it. Not taking it away, but giving us the strength and courage to bear it. This is a fact about my experience repetitively, not just with mild pain but also with the most severe levels of pain that I have experienced.

Again and again, grace comes and shows me that, through acceptance, surrender and allowing severe physical pain to simply be here, something more comes. That something more is a mystery — a vast and great presence that can hold the pain. It holds it with care, with love, and with complete and utter compassion. That is the balm we need to live well with pain.

We need to do our part though; our part in living well with the pain is to practice cooperating with the pain as life brings it. We do all we can to alleviate it; we take our medications, we follow our programme of things that we know will help us. In case none of the above works, the most important thing we can do is to surrender and cooperate with life which is showing up as pain.

Chapter 1

❦

How to Leverage Your Emotional Pain for Peace and Prosperity

essie Naranjo, a sociologist from the Tewa Village of Santa Clara, summed up an inner longing for peace and absence of pain when she observed: "It's the most precious thing to know absolutely where you belong. There's a whole emotional wrapping-around-of-you-here. You see the same rock, tree, road, clouds, sun — you develop a nice kind of intimacy with the world around you. To be intimate is to grow, to learn... [it] is absolutely fulfilling. Intimacy, that's my magic word..."

The Question of Belonging

As we examine the first steps to leverage emotional pain, we have to come to the center. This may be the most important question you should ask yourself. Where do you belong? Why? Are you deliberate about that choice? And is it what you dream of for your life? A friend recently confessed to me:

"I married at a very young age. Now that there are so many demands in my life, and I'm matured, I realized this is far away from what my soul craves. I am not who I should be."

Her dream? To attend college and become a nurse. Her reality? In rural America, four children, low income, high debt, strained relationship with spouse. Counseling isn't going well, not because they don't love each other — they do. It's just grown to a state of near catatonic responsibility. Can it be revived? Perhaps, if they both find the place where they veered apart and begin to communicate, but even then, it'll be pretty tough. Truth? They are staying together for their children's sake. Is there pain? Yes. . .not from loss but from the lack of fulfillment, from dreams that slipped into the cracks of busy life, lack of planning, and no real goals. I go back to this question that I asked her, "Where do you belong?" If you don't know where you're going, it makes no difference which road you take. So what arc your goals and where do you belong?

Emotional pain and who we are has deep roots in this question of belonging. So our belonging might be reactive to needs that were borne in us as children, young adults, persons who are married, or divorced. The challenge is: do you know what you really want in life? I don't mean a new dream or hope that is pinned on emotion or desire. In the core of your person, what and who are you called to be? Emotional pain often limits our ability to dream, and doubt our possibilities by saying: "you were nothing before, you will be nothing forever. You can never be anything more than___." Once you fill in that blank with your deep pain, you're going to be able to acknowledge that you are not limited by your past. I don't care if you got a GED five years after your graduating class, you can still achieve a PhD, if that is your calling.

LIFE PRINCIPLE: Nothing that you dream, imagine, work for, is impossible unless you believe it is. Without faith, even the most simple moments become unobtainable in life.

Ending Emotional Pain: Understanding the Belonging

Use a clean sheet of paper, get yourself a pencil and a calm and a clear space where you can focus for few minutes. Where do you belong? Try to answer in terms of need for this exercise, not specifics like: "I belong with my child at home." Okay, it's a fact that those of us who are married or parents may say "I belong with ———." That is not what we're looking for. What we're striving to see is that reality for which you pray and believe; those forming dreams and goals for the future. Here is my example:

"I belong in a world where listening is important, and there is a high value on human need in the eyes of faith. I belong in the place where I can trust the man that I love from the depths of my heart and back again, knowing that his word is as reliable as my own heartbeat. I belong in a town where people know one another, speak at the grocery, laugh and cry. I belong in a workspace that allows me to connect with my own creativity, to write, to talk with people about life, and to learn constantly. I belong in a physical space that is solid, filled with nature, unique, and historical. I belong to a faith that is not condemning nor accusing, but will still love me enough to speak the truth, and for me specifically—the truth in Christ. I belong to a sensual intimacy with the one person who shares my most intimate thoughts, my most intimate moments, all of my dreams, and all of his as well. I belong in a world permeated by faith, hope and love; surrounded by people who breathe possibility into their own dreams as well."

Without these things, I experience emotional pain in my daily life. If I act in violation of these basic belonging needs, my anxiety will rise, emotional pain will increase, and I will react by experiencing decreased joy and happiness. So, the question becomes inherently important on how you react to life on a daily basis, and how you react to emotional pain caused by outside sources. Emotional pain is sometimes a warning signal as well. It may be telling you that you are isolating or robbing yourself of a place of intimacy and you have to change the way you deal with an altered reality. This leads us back to the place of emotional pain from outside circumstances.

Letting Go

The concept of letting go is overused in our society,; the idea of "closure" without the work that goes behind it. Until you allow the pain of your loss to come into your soul, feel the authenticity of it, acknowledge its presence, then you will be able to take the step of healing and faith of "letting go." Let's put this scenario of attachment as a snapshot so we can all understand; a word picture to get the point across.

Imagine being in a comfortable room where you have history. Then you look around and the comfort is no longer there; the room is decayed, and the floor is flooded with ice-cold water. It's dark with shadows that you are not comfortable with, though the light still has a little golden to it. The temperature is unkind to you, and no matter what you do, there is no comfort to be found. You see little flashes here and there when the sun rises for just a moment, and you are able to feel the warmth through the window. As soon as that moment of emotional sunlight passes, you are back into the darkness of waiting for a change that is not going to come.

You go to the door and feel the panic — you can't take what was in that room with you. "His" memory is there, "her" memory is there, and your history is there. It's what you know. You try to reach for the handle but feel panic in your chest. You go back to the soggy couch, reviewing the scenes on the walls as well as the photographs in your heart. You replay your story, the promises that used to fill this space. Your mind knows that leaving the room is the best option, for there are many rooms in the world waiting to fill your life with grace, make you feel loved, and treat you with respect and dignity. Some of the terrain between rooms is tough and you're afraid to leave where you are. It's been what you know, and it wasn't always this way nor this hard. But you're tired of being alone and cold in the dark. You long for the sun and warmth on your face for more than a moment.

Relationship loss is a lot like this. Those who are left often tend to wait in the room that has fallen apart, not realizing that the relationship cannot be restored to what it "used to be." Those married people who reunite after any form of separation have found that they need to fall in love again with the changed person they were once married to a long time ago.

Turning the Knob

How do you get away from the emotional pain and move pass the haunting loss to the peace and prosperity? How do you grasp the handle? First, realize that pain in some ways is your friend. It's telling you that something has to change. If you're a male or female constantly in emotional pain in your life, your mind and heart are desperately trying to tell you something. Determining what that is, is the real trick.

First, don't treat pain as a single instance, rather, look for the source. If you recently became single, avoid the idea of: "It's because she left me." Although rejection is painful, it's not the source of the pain. The pain comes from something more; like fear of failure in relationship, missing the intimacy that was shared, a need for love and acceptance that has been stunted. Most relationships that end don't do so in a vacuum so most of us have time to process — long before the final split takes place. Perhaps your pain comes from being cheated on by the person you still live with. Again, the real pain is the loss of trust and faith that ought to be life long, even when forgiveness is present. For this reason, less than thirty percent of couples who experience infidelity remain together for a long time, especially when the issues are not properly resolved in counseling.

The step in letting go is to:

    A. Know where you belong: Have a sense of self that is not reliant on anyone else, what people think of you or on social pressures.

Know thyself.

B. Recognize your game state: This is life, not a test. I know that it's hard to do, but take a serious life assessment minus any real drama. For instance, write out those dreams and goals that support your "belonging". How does this life mirror the one that you live?

C. Recognize relational breakdowns for what they are: I had to return to a time in my life which happened to be captured on a video tape when I was teaching a class. I watched myself teach for an hour. Realizing it on that day, I was happy and well. The person that hurt me so badly later in life was already out there and the world simply continued spinning around. Not only was the universe fine without his presence, so was I. My painful friendship was not worth what it was costing me in self-esteem or damage to possibilities I could conceive. Dreaming had become dependent on another person, not on faith.

LIFE PRINCIPLE: When you rely on another person to "make" you happy, you have chosen to fail. Happiness comes from within you; it is your responsibility.

J. Donald Walters once said: "Happiness is not a brilliant climax to years of grim struggle and anxiety. It is a long succession of little decisions simply to be happy in the moment." This is how we turn the door knob to the room — that is attachment — the first step in letting go. It's on bleeding knees that we rise up from our place of weeping (crawl if necessary) to the opening in the wall. We throw open the door knowing that every little decision of health and wellness takes you one step closer to the edge of the tree line, out of the forest and into the sun.

Chapter 2

✑

How to Live in Peace Despite Suffering in The World

There are terrible events happening all around the planet. How can mindfulness help with the sadness, helplessness or insecurity generated by all these events?

This is a big question that many ask in the context of meditation. When you watch the news on television, you get the impression that there is so much bad in the world. One may wonder whether the situation has gotten worse or whether our awareness of what is happening has progressed to the point where we are now. This takes nothing away from all the horrific events and suffering that people can experience.

There are some disconcerting truths about meditation that are rarely discussed. Meditation has nothing to do with the development of strength, it is rather an embrace to vulnerability. It's not a reinforcement of control, it's letting go. It is not the status quo, it is the acceptance of impermanence. This is not to maintain the suffering of others at a distance, it is getting closer little by little. As disconcerting as it may seem, it is these qualities that bring a healthier and happier spirit.

When we hear the atrocities happening around the world, it's hard not to be upset. It is important to be clear with yourself at this point if you feel pain like genuine empathy or if this pain is just an emotional reaction created by your mind as there are many every day.

For example, a person can listen to the news on

television and feel a wave of sadness or pain for his fellow human beings. Allowing this wave of sadness to overwhelm him will leave him plenty of time to dissipate. We could say that it is to allow the mind to be such, that is, without adding anything.

For some people, hearing the same news on television makes them feel a wave of sadness, making it their own. A person like this cultivates sadness by thinking about it over and over again, although it is beyond his control.

Therefore, if we do not ignore or resist what's going on, we will just be with what's going on. Of course, the more critical the situation is, the more difficult it is to maintain a state of stable mindfulness. But like any other skill, with practice and repetition, we can become more familiar with this process and better in our abilities.

Out of context, it may seem cold enough and even far from the pains of others. In fact, it is quite the opposite of connecting to the suffering of others as it is without projection, distraction and judgments; simply by opening one's heart.

It may seem too passive for some. But this is actually just the opposite. By clearly seeing the reality, we become much more capable of discerning where we can make a real difference; not just being grumpy and angry, but proactively moving forward whenever the opportunity arises — only then can one appropriately help other people.

This clarity allows us to see how these events impact our inner world and daily lives. We start by seeing that fear is natural and impermanent, and we do not need to adhere to it even if the media tries to convince us otherwise. When we fully experience fear, we understand how hard it is for those who live with it all the time, and we are more likely to feel empathy. And it is very difficult to be caught by our own insecurities when we are focused on improving the happiness of others.

Chapter 3

❦

How to Stop Living in the Hurt

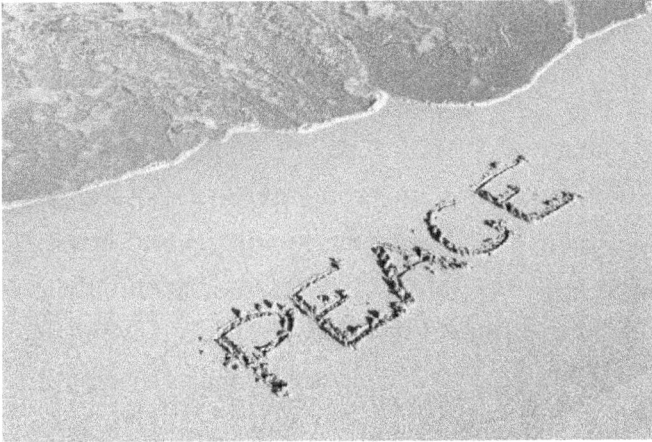

We have all felt hurt at some point in our lives. No matter how old you are, you have at some point experienced some emotional pain.

It hurts. I get it.

But what you do with that wound is probably more important than the pain itself. Would you prefer to be an active part of life again? Or do you prefer to search endlessly for the past? The past is something that cannot be changed.

In short, how do we put aside the wounds of the past and move on? Here, we'll discover it.

Blaming others for our pain is what most of us do at the beginning. Someone did something bad to us, or they offended us in some way that mattered to us. We want them to apologize. We want them to recognize what they did was wrong.

But blaming others for our pain can be counterproductive. The problem with blaming others is that it can often leave you powerless. For example, you face that person (your boss, your spouse, your parents, your son...), and they say, "No, I did not do it" or worse; "And what if I did it?" Then you will accumulate anger and pain with no resolution.

All your feelings are legitimate. It is important to feel full and then move on. Accumulating complaints indefinitely is a bad habit because it hurts you more than it hurts them.

People who cling to these hurts of the past often relive the pain over and over again. Sometimes, a person can even get "stuck" in this pain or guilt.

Five ways to heal the wounds of the past

The only way you can heal is to accept new joy and happiness into your life and make room for it. If your heart is full of pain, how can you be open to anything new?

1. Make the decision of letting go

Things do not disappear by themselves. You have to commit to "let it go." If you do not make this conscious choice in advance, you could end up sabotaging any effort to let go of this pain from the past.

2. Express your pain and your responsibility

Express what pain makes you feel, either directly to the other person, or simply to a friend, write it in a diary, or write a letter that you will never send to the other person. Doing so will also help you understand what your pain is about.

What can you do differently next time? Are you an active participant in your own life or simply a victim without hope? Are you going to let your pain become your identity? Or are you someone deeper and more complex than that?

3. Stop being the victim and blame others

Being a victim makes you feel good; it's like

being on the winning team against the world. But you know what? To a large extent, the world does not care; therefore, you need to get more of yourself. Yes, you are special. Yes, your feelings are important, but do not get confused between "your feelings." "Your feelings should nullify all things, and nothing else should matter."

Your feelings are just one part of this great thing that we call life, which is complex and disorderly.

You need to take responsibility for your own happiness and not put so much power in the hands of another person. Why let the person who hurt you in the past have such power, right here, at this moment?

4. Focus on the present (the here and now) and current joy

Now is the time to let go of your past and stop reliving it. You cannot undo the past; all you can do is make the best day of your life today.

When you focus on the present, you will have less time to think about the past. When the memories of the past slide into your consciousness (since they are bound to appear from time to time), identify them; then focus on the present again.

Remember, if we squeeze our brains and live with feelings of pain, there is little room for something positive. It is a decision you must make: Welcome joy into your life again.

5. Forgive them

We may not have to forget the bad behavior of another person, but almost everyone deserves forgiveness. Sometimes, we get stuck in our pain and our stubbornness that we cannot even imagine forgiveness. Forgiveness is not saying, "I agree with what you did." Or "It's Ok." No. Instead, it is, "I do not agree with what you did, but I forgive you anyway."

Forgiveness is not a sign of weakness. Instead, it is simply saying: "I am a good person. You deserve forgiveness. You did something that hurt me, but I want to move forward in my life and feel the joy again. I cannot do that completely until I let go of the pain."

Forgiveness is a way of empathizing with the other person and trying to see things from their perspective.

Forgiving yourself can be an important part of this step, just as, at times, we may come to blame ourselves for the situation or harm. If you cannot forgive yourself, how will you live peacefully and happily in the future?

So, to move on in your life or let go of the past and the pain it caused, forgive yourself and forgive others.

I know that it is incredibly difficult to put aside one's pain. If we have stayed in it for a long time, it feels like an old friend's pain. The pain is justified, and it would be a sacrilege to let it go.

Nobody's life should be defined by their pain. It is not healthy as it adds to our stress, affects our ability to concentrate on study and work and every other relationship we have. Every day you choose to cling to pain is another day when everyone around you has to live with that decision and feel its consequences.

Let go of the pain. Do something different today, and happiness will come into your life again.

Chapter 4

❦

How to Relieve the Feeling of Emptiness

Most people, throughout their lives, sometimes experience the so-called feeling of emptiness, which is usually located in the upper part of the stomach. Emotions, such as loneliness, anguish, frustration, despair, etc., are usually accompanied by this sensation. The feeling of emptiness is often accompanied by other feelings such as rejection or abandonment.

Some people may suffer this sensation more frequently and may trigger a strong lack of control in both emotion and behavior — appearing more impulsive in behaviors. For example, in cases of depressive syndromes, it is very common for people to experience borderline personality disorder or emotional dependence. This feeling is not easy to handle, and it creates strong emotions and existential pain.

If the feeling of emptiness is not adequately addressed, it is possible for the person to rush to escape and end their suffering. They adopt various mechanisms — such as blaming others for their situation, indulging in substance use, feeding problems, reckless behavior, kleptomania, pathological gambling, uncontrolled sexual relations, and many more — which eventually undermines their self-esteem and physical integrity. All this will bring new problems to the person, almost with total insecurity, which can aggravate that feeling of emptiness, thus, closing a dangerous and pernicious circle.

In therapy, it is important to detect if the person suffers from this sensation. Also, the frequency and the ability of such a person to cope with it and how to mitigate it are to be detected. It is also important to empower the person to cope with one of the sensations that most pain, suffering, and lack of control causes in human beings.

HOW CAN THE VACUUM FEELING BE RELIEVED?

The trap of self-disqualification

Many people have been able to verify during their childhood and their life that when they disqualified themselves, they received support from the people who accompanied them, which minimized their self-criticism and enhanced their positive aspects. In the end, this behavior can be automated and resort to inertia. In the most serious cases, self-deprecation leads to self-harm and suicide attempts as a wake-up call because the more the person uses this, the more vulnerable resource is the absence of the person (s) who comforts him or her.

Anticipate the company

One technique that can help anticipate the company is the so-called "neighbor's technique." This technique is an imagination of a person suffering from the feeling of emptiness. The person suffering will imagine that a relative, a friend, or a neighbor knocks on his door and explain to them who is suffering from a situation like them. In the next step, the person will imagine what he would say to this neighbor to help remember what could help him/her in past situations.

Autoacompañamiento

Anticipating the company is intended to progressively help the person to maintain an internal dialogue of self-regulation. To overcome the feeling of emptiness and be able to give the attention needed, to reduce effective dependence.

Improve self-concept

- Self-esteem: Improving the way a person communicates with him/herself is fundamental. We learn to relate with ourselves in our younger days; this depends on how others have talked to us. Thus, over time, different "voices" appear in our heads that chat with each other. When these voices devalue us, we can have a problem with self-esteem. Therefore, it is essential to affix and change pathological criticism.

- Self-image: It is important to relate appropriately with our body and create a personal image with which we feel comfortable. Today, the "ideal image" is mediated by stereotypes and myths that are not easy to overcome since we are bombarded with it from our earliest childhood. A healthy relationship between our body and our image improves our self-concept and decreases the likelihood of suffering from the dreaded feeling of emptiness.

- **Self-efficacy:** Learning to set desired life goals, describing problems in a manageable way, and finding solutions to life's difficulties that do not go against one's values are efficient ways to improve a person's perception of the effectiveness of their actions. For this, you may need (1) training in solving problems,(2) to avoid problems and uncomfortable emotions that can arise when you think of a solution (especially when it does not come out as easy as you would have imagined).

Be aware of your strengths

When a person suffers from the feeling of emptiness, he may not know or disregard the positive aspects of his personality. It is normal to focus more on their "shortcomings," which surely perceive them as extended and very difficult to change. We all have strengths and weaknesses due to our human condition, so it is very positive that they know and cultivate their strengths. The VIA questionnaire of 24 strengths of character is very suitable for this.

Project purpose/values/meaning of your life

Creating a vital project with objectives to direct yourself and choose how you want to achieve them can help the person construct the purpose or the meaning of their existence. The inner journey that one undertakes when trying to answer these questions or appropriate ways to experience joy and peace is also a way of responding to inner emptiness.

Enrich social relationships

Cultivating relationships with others is an excellent way to get to know one another better and connect with the world. We are social beings, and if we are deprived of this fundamental aspect of the human being, we are preparing the ground for the feeling of emptiness to appear.

Allow yourself to enjoy and reward yourself based on the effort and not the results

Performing activities that you are passionate about — enjoying the process, rewarding the effort you made without focusing on the results — is a great way to fill our lives with what really matters to us. And in the end, it is shown as the best way to get the results you want.

Although it is sometimes hard to self-observe the feeling of emptiness, it is important to investigate inwardly where that pain might come from to choose the solution(s) or the most appropriate attitude.

Chapter 5

∝

HowTo Relieve the Feeling of Emptiness as a way to peace and prosperity

Many of us experience emptiness at some juncture in our lives, but not many can recognize precisely why they feel this way.

We blame insufficient purpose, a lost lover, not

enough friends, or other reasons, but this only dodges around the true reason for emptiness.

Nonetheless, none of these reasons get to the real cause of why people feel empty; Honestly, now, we have so much uncertainty and destruction in the world because people feel this emptiness, and they look outside themselves to fix it. Or, out of resentment and aloneness, they hurt others to release these feelings. None of this will resolve the problem, though. At the heart of emptiness lies an absence of love for oneself.

Our fear of emptiness and our failed efforts to manage it are at the root of our suffering in relationships, finances, and health.

Our personalities are wired to believe that there isn't enough. Not enough love, not enough money, not enough happiness – our fear of emptiness keeps us in struggle and turmoil. When we embrace and confront, emptiness becomes a treasure to be valued rather than an enemy.

We have to get to a place and say that enough is enough. We are not alone here. With us, inside us, is the perfect wordless presence. (love)

Our hearts' proper understanding is revealed in the clarity we discover when we look within. To find the greater self, we don't have to give up ourselves we only need to trust and dig deep. The abundance we gain by learning how to love ourselves contains a lot of love and happiness.

Emptiness, when confronted, brings us the harmony and wholeness we've been looking for, striving for, and trying to achieve in the world.

Emptiness creates room for confidence, which we sometimes lack in our busy lives. Emptiness is the peace and love that our anxious minds crave.

I've experienced that emptiness more than I ever wanted to. In my case, the proximal cause was constant rejection from loved ones and society. However, I think it goes much further than that. My self-esteem and confidence in who I was and could be was non-existent.

I kept hearing and reading that only I could fill that emptiness. I could look around outside, but in the end, I was the only one who could fill it. As you probably know, that appeared like an impossible task.

Nothing seemed like it would fill the emptiness: I certainly didn't have that love for myself. How could I? I had never been adequate in my entire life, and I had tried hard. I honestly wasn't good enough. Not enough entrepreneurial spirit. Not enough confidence. Not good-looking enough. Not talented enough. Not lovable enough. Or so I thought!

Despite the emptiness, I still kept trying. Out of desperation, I would reach out to men and external situations, hoping for love, and at times I would find temporary joy. The affairs were lacking. They lasted a month, on average, but still, it took away the emptiness.

There can only be one aspect that fills the emptiness, and that is love. A lack of love for oneself is the major cause of inner emptiness. However, this is not due to someone else's love — it is due to not loving yourself. "

Emptiness itself can make you feel as though you have a hole in your heart, as an element is missing. All your interests, aspirations, and joyful moments become meaningless to you. Contrary to what is believed, feeling empty need not mean you are depressed. Instead, it makes you miss that feeling of being miserable, considering it would imply you are experiencing something, that you are alive. Alternatively, you don't feel gratified, either you can't feel any emotion - all you can anticipate is apathy.

Besides, this feeling of emptiness can last for a long time if untreated, yet you have the power within you to change. We have phases, much like the moon. Phases in which emptiness is necessary to be complete and shine as bright as we can. Even though there is nothing crueler than losing yourself, you need to take action to find yourself again, and above all, remind yourself that these phases are temporary. They are a moment of realization.

Now that we know lack of self-love leads to empty feelings, how do we handle it?

The following are four ways in which you can replenish the loneliness in your life:

1. Dig Deep into your feelings

We will only solve the problem when we first understand it. What prevents you from enjoying yourself thoroughly? Ripping out your wounds and learning to love your scars requires courage, but it is a necessary step on the way to self-love.

It will not happen overnight, but you must confront your ego and show it, love, at some point. Then there will be nothing left to pine for and nothing to take away from you.

Of course, losing someone you care about or

going through a devastating experience can lead to feelings of emptiness, which is understandable. Please take note, consistent feelings of emptiness, however, can mean something more profound to you.

2. PERMIT YOUR EMOTIONS TO EXPRESS THEMSELVES

No one should go through life suppressing all your emotions. This isn't only unhealthy; it's even unnatural. We are emotional beings with various feelings, and we should not be forced to suppress them merely because culture tends to frown on people who do so. Do whatever it takes to make you feel more whole inside yourself.

Do something that comes naturally to you, whether writing, singing, hiking, painting, or dancing,

Any of the above will help fill that gap and give you a sound outlet for your emotions.

3. STAY COMMITTED AND AGREE TO LOVE YOURSELF

Listen, I struggle with this sometimes; I can assure you that loving yourself is a serious challenge because we are taught to put others before ourselves. We have every excuse in the world to love ourselves, but most of us do not feel worthy enough when it comes to it. We can log in on social media at any time and constantly compare ourselves.

We can watch TV commercials that promise to make us "perfect," or we can listen to negative people that discredit and dismiss us. However, we can choose to ignore all this and commit to loving ourselves unconditionally.

And so the question is, How do you go about doing this? You make a choice.

Choose to love yourself regardless of what other people think of you, choose to love yourself through whatever mistakes you make, and decide to love yourself regardless of what path you take in life. You can't truly live life if you can't appreciate and love the person with whom you spend the most time, and that person is yourself.

4. Do ACTIVITIES THAT MAKE YOU HAPPY.

Participating in activities that make your heart grateful goes a long way against encountering emptiness in your life. You will not even notice a void in your life if you fill it with activities that make you happy. Even if you have been knocked down, you can always get back up.

Instead of succumbing to feelings of worthlessness and loss, you can still choose to fight back.

- Do at least 1 fun activity at work per day, and include your co-workers
- Register for a yoga course
- Pick up a hobby or activity again that you used to enjoy when you were a child or teenager.
- Learn how to cook a healthy meal that you never cooked before.
- join a reading club
- Be grateful
- Improve lighting in your house so each room is adapted to the mood you would most like to have.
- Write something nice on the bathroom mirror for your significant other each day.
- Spend 30 days putting any friend or family member in a better emotional state as when you found them
- get together with friends

Do whatever it takes to make you happy. And when you start replacing those feelings with love, the emptiness disappears gradually.

Know that life necessitates continuous movement for us to survive. Emptiness's biggest enemies are momentum and action.

Now, let's tie in peace and Prosperity

what is peace to you?

For me peace is about harmony, within myself and with others around me. It does not necessarily mean 'having it my way but all the more about acceptance and being okay with how things are.

There are two sides to any coin. Peace is serene, but it instills in us a sense of inspiration. Peace breaks down walls while bolstering our inner spirit. Peace may be the difference between dying and living entirely. Peace both declutters and encumbers the mind.

You must examine yourself and sort out the inconsistencies. If you want to be transparent about your work here on earth, you must be completely honest with yourself and build understanding.

Every human beings strive for peace and prosperity in their lives.

One of the keys to peace is self-reflection.

Looking in the mirror and explaining what you see is self-reflection. Many people find self-reflection daunting because it requires them to examine their positive, negative, and indifference from deep inside. They don't understand why they require it, and they don't see the advantages of doing so.

Self-reflection is important for self-awareness because it helps us to look at ourselves objectively.

When the inner man is disrupted, peace cannot exist. And I agree that achieving harmony is the key to tying together all of the elements we've been discussing thus far .

Peace isn't the absence of uncertainty and problems; rather, it's the ability to remain calm, centered, and unified in the face of them.

What is Prosperity to you?

When you hear the word "money," what comes to mind? A large amount of money, valuable possessions, and land. Although the word prosperity is a clear, specific word that can be used as a noun or a verb, it implies a bright future. Furthermore, the word "prosper" means "to survive" or "to cause to succeed."

I did a poll and Most people I polled answered that question like this:

"Prosperity is described as a state of growth,

thriving, good fortune, and/or social success. Prosperity mostly refers to money, but it often refers to other variables such as happiness and health, which can be independent of wealth to varying degrees."

Prosperity aids in maintaining a happy state, but it does not guarantee happiness.

There are numerous stories that show how a beggar can live a happy and content life while a king can have riches but be miserable and unsatisfied.

Prosperity is a measure of the amount of personal effort needed to maintain one's well-being, such as comfort, health, and family support.

I believe that prosperity founded solely on the acquisition of riches, strength, status, and wealth is unstable and may lead to a "false sense of prosperity." The reason for this is that our sense of well-being can be shattered when we are confronted with sickness, death, or disempowerment.

So my idea of prosperity is fostering a deeply rooted "inner peace" that is founded on the concrete foundation of living a life of intention, meaning, doing the right thing, and love, rather than the fragile foundations of materialism and status. And being able to meet our "basic" physical and psychological needs in order to keep going.

Here what I've discovered to help me balance emptiness, harmony, and prosperity in my life.

Setting Personal Goals

Setting goals is essential for success in any endeavor. Turn your abundant vision into clearly defined goals. The goals must be precise and summarized in a way that you understand exactly what you want to achieve. Be straightforward on what you intend to accomplish. Don't just say you want to get in shape or be healthier. Make it a specific target that you can monitor. What's more, if you achieve your goals on a consistent basis, the strategy you have in place and the process you use to achieve them will become a habit. Each new challenge you complete will make the next one even more simple. The excitement and rush of success never wears off; instead, each achievement piques your interest in taking on new and exciting challenges.

You need Dedication with Motivation

There isn't anything humanly possible that you can't do with motivation. But motivation only goes so far. To be committed to something, you must be able to make sacrifices and set aside the time required to achieve it. Dedication is what will get you through the difficult times and ensure that you complete the process. For example, you may be really motivated to lose weight, but you may never achieve your target until you develop the willpower to get off the couch and go for a jog.

According to studies, willpower can be built by perseverance. With its support, you'll be able to overcome your shortcomings and faults, as well as develop your self-limiting habits.

Take Action with Hard Work

Its going to take hard work to make your vision a reality. you must be able to put all of your energies, abilities, and skills to work. Working hard is only way to succeed in this life. You can't do anything if you don't take action. Your dreams will come true if you take action. It is also behavior that allows plans to become a reality. It's not enough to just think and plan. The difference between winners and losers is action – specifically, continuous action. And you can do it if you put forth a great deal of effort. There are no short cuts.

Make Positive People Connections

You'll need people to inspire and help you while you pursue your dreams, wishes, and goals.

You should also seek the advice and insights of experts on how to proceed with the realization of your dreams.

Establish connections with positive people and professionals who can provide you with information, expertise, and solutions, as well as stand by your side during difficult times. But keep in mind that you aren't looking for validation from them because you have already validated yourself.

It's okay to seek their assistance when you need it, and make an effort to assist them whenever possible so that your relationships aren't one-sided.

Optimistic Perseverance

Perseverance is the product of a mixture of habits and a positive mental attitude. Having the desire to persevere isn't enough unless it's accompanied by the optimism to do so. Grit necessitates not only inspiration but also volition. To turn your intentions into actions, you'll need mental toughness.

People who are successful do not give up easily. They recognize that having dreams, hopes, aspirations, and a vision isn't enough to achieve success in life. It is necessary to keep trying and doing until success is achieved. Take note that failures and disappointments are common in the pursuit of fulfillment.

It is critical to confront your losses in order to understand who you are, what you can overcome, and how to move forward.

Chapter 6

How to Overcome Grief and Pain

When you lose someone or something dear to you, your sorrow can be immense. Pain, bad memories, and unanswered questions may come to haunt you. You might even feel like you will never be the same person again or that you will never be able to laugh or be whole again. Rely on your courage, even if there is no way to grieve without pain; there are healthy ways to grieve that allow you to move forward constructively. Do not resign yourself to a life without happiness.

Bear the grief

- Facing the loss: After a significant loss, we sometimes want to do something, anything, to ease the pain. By indulging in a harmful habit, for example, taking drugs, drinking alcohol, staying too long in bed, using the Internet more than necessary, or engaging in shameless sex, you are threatening your well-being. This may leave you vulnerable to addictions and other sufferings. You will never really heal until you deal with your loss. You will not be able to ignore the pain caused by the loss or anesthetize yourself with distractions for a very long time. Even if you do everything in your power to escape, your grief will catch up. Face your loss, give yourself permission to cry or mourn naturally. Only by recognizing your grief will you be able to fight it.

When a loss is still fresh in your memory, your

sorrow deserves your full attention. However, you should avoid feeling this sorrow for too long. Give yourself some time, maybe a few days or a week, to be deeply sad. Prolonged indulgence holds you a prisoner of the feeling of loss — paralyzed by pity for yourself and unable to move forward.

- Let your pain out, and let the tears flow: do not be afraid to cry, even if it's not something you normally do. Understand that there is no right way to feel pain or express it. The most important thing is to recognize this pain and try to overcome it. You choose the way and understand how to do it. Individuals' way of overcoming pain differs from person to person; therefore, do not expect yours to be like others.

- Find an outlet for your pain: If you want to do some activity during your mourning period, do it, but make sure it is not harmful to you or others. You can cry, pound into your pillow, go running, throw things on the ground, drive for a long time, scream as hard as you can in a forest or some other place where you'd be alone, or crunch your memories — these are some ways that people find to bring out their pain. All these ways are helpful.

- Express your feelings in front of friends: It is healthy to look for people who will take care of you when you are suffering. If you cannot find a friend, contact a compassionate stranger, priest, counselor, or therapist. If you feel that you are confused and unsure of yourself, talking to someone you trust can eliminate some of your pain. See the discussion as a form of storage for your emotions. Note that your thoughts do not need to be coherent or reasoned; they must only be expressive. If you are concerned that people who listen to you may feel confused or upset by what you are saying, you could relieve those concerns by warning them at the beginning. Just let them know that you feel sad and you would like to have someone to talk to; and that even though some of the words you are going to say may not make sense, you appreciate their listening ears. Listen! It will not matter to a friend who cares about you or someone who supports you whether your statements make sense or not.

- Stay away from people who do not show compassion: Unfortunately, not everyone you talk to during your time of grief will help you. Ignore people who tell you things like: "stop being so sensitive," "I moved on quickly when the same thing happened to me," and so on. They do not know how you feel. So, do not pay attention to their dismissive comments. Tell them that they do not have to see you during this period if it's too much for them. You have to go through this time, so just ask them to give you space.

Some people who disdain your grief may even be friends with good intentions (but misguided). Reconnect with them when you feel stronger. Until then, take your distance from their impatience; you cannot be in haste to feel better emotionally.

- Do not feed on regret: After losing someone, you may feel guilty and blame yourself. Or you may be worried about thoughts like I wish I had said goodbye one last time or would have liked to behave better with him. Do not be consumed by guilt; neither should you blame yourself. You cannot change the past by constantly dwelling in it. It would not be your fault if you lost a loved one. Rather than constantly thinking about what might have happened or should have happened, focus on what you can do now; treat your emotions, and move on.

If you feel guilty after experiencing this loss, talk to others who knew this person or the object of your loss. They will almost always be able to convince you that it was not your fault.

- Keep things that remind you of your lost loved one: The departure of a person or pet doesn't mean you wouldn't remember them anymore. It can be comforting to know that even if that person is no longer there, the friendship, the love, or personal connection that you always had still existed. Nobody will ever be able to take it from you, and your relationship will always be there with you. Some memories will always be worth remembering for your own courage, tenacity, and the ability to envision a better future.

Keep the memories that remind you of this person or your pet in a box at a place where you will not see it every day. Take it out when you need a tangible reminder of your memories. In general, it is better not to leave those memories in a place where you can see them every time; a constant reminder that a person is no more makes it hard to move on.

- Get help: There is an excessively hurtful brand of infamy against people who have emotional problems in our society. You will not be weak or pathetic if you consult a therapist or counselor. On the contrary, it is a sign of strength. By asking for help, you show an admirable desire to move on and overcome your grief. Do not hesitate to make an appointment with a professional.

- Work to achieve happiness: Move your center of attention away from your sadness. Try to remember the good times and the best memories you shared with that person or with the pet you had. You will not change what happened by focusing on negative thoughts or regrets. It will only make things worse. Be sure that a person who has brought you happiness would not want you to indulge in sadness. Try to remember some things, such as how that person spoke, those weird ways, the moments you shared, the laughs you shared with them, and the things that person taught you about life and yourself.

If you have lost your pet, remember the happy

times you spent together, the happy life you gave your pet, and his special character.

Whenever you feel tempted to be sad, angry, or pity yourself, take a diary and write the good things you can remember about that person or the object of your loss. When you feel sad, you can check your diary to remember the joy you have felt.

- Find a distraction: By staying busy and doing tasks that require concentration, you can take a break from your grief. It also gives you enough space to realize that there are still good things in life.

Even though work and study can relieve you of constant thoughts about your loss, do not just rely on your daily life to distract yourself or risk living a life of work and sadness without anything in between. Re-focus on happier goals by doing something that makes you feel at peace; there are many possibilities, for example, gardening, cooking, fishing, listening to your favorite songs, strolling, drawing, painting, writing, etc. Choose an activity that gives you joy and makes you calm down (it is not something that works or studies can always give you).

- Consider social work: Move your concentration from your own problems to the problems of others. Consider volunteering. If you love children, you could calm your mind by helping young children who are very spontaneous and laugh a lot.

- Find pleasure in each of your days: When you have overcome your initial sadness, take the opportunity to enjoy the sunny days. Spend time walking, contemplating, and simply observing the natural beauty around you. Do not try to feel any particular feelings — just let the heat of the sun flood you and the sounds of the world go through you—Marvel at the beauty of the trees and the architecture you see. Let the hustle and bustle of life remind you that the world is beautiful. Life goes on, you deserve to be a part of it, and you will eventually return to your daily life.

There is scientific evidence that sunlight is a natural anti-depressant. You could recover from your loss by leaving your home and taking some sunlight.

- Get the idea of what you lost: When you lose someone, it is an unfortunate fact that you will never be able to enjoy his physical presence ever again. However, this does not mean that this person or this domestic animal does not exist in this world in the form of memories or actions. Know that the object of your loss still lives in your memory, in your thoughts, in your words, and your actions. When you say, do, or think of something influenced by that person's memory, they continue to live. Many religions teach that the soul or essence of a person remains after the death of his physical body. Other religions teach that this essence is transformed into another form or redistributed on Earth. If you are a practitioner, find solace by telling yourself that the person you lost still exists in a spiritual sense.

- Spend time with people who do you good: It can be difficult to motivate yourself to go out or spend time with friends after a loss. However, this can help you improve your mood. It is good to look for the company of your friends who can understand your emotional state, even if you have not yet recovered 100%. Find friends or acquaintances with whom you can have fun but who will always be friendly and sensitive to your situation. They will help you resume your normal social role, which in return can help keep you busy while you are doing your grieving. The first release after a significant loss can be a little dark or weird just because your friends are worried about how to approach the subject. Do not let this demoralize you; you have to re-enter a normal social life at some time. Do not be discouraged, even if you need weeks or months to feel completely normal; spending time with your friends is always a good idea.

- Do not pretend to be happy: As you return to your usual activities, you may feel that some group situations require you to be happier than you are. Even if you must avoid complacency in your sorrow, you must also avoid forcing happiness. Forced happiness is a horrible thing. Forcing a smile when you do not want to is a real burden. Do not make your happiness a chore! There is no problem if you want to look serious in your social life and work, as long as you do nothing to prevent others' happiness. Keep your smile for the times when you feel really happy; it will be much softer.

- Give yourself time to heal: Time heals all wounds. Your emotional recovery can take months or years; that's normal. Then when it's time, you can begin to honor the lost person's memory by deciding once again to enjoy life to its fullest.

- Do not worry; you will never forget the people you have loved: You will never lose the strength that has led you to your lost goals. What could change is how you approach life from then on; you could focus better, have a new perspective on your values, or a completely changed perspective on certain aspects of your life. However, this progress will not be possible if you do not give yourself time to heal.

Although you must give yourself enough time to heal, at the same time, it is important to remember that your life is a precious thing, and you are responsible for getting the most out of it. The purpose of all existence is to be happy, not unhappy. Do not rush out of your sorrow, but do not settle for a partial recovery. Make your journey towards healing and gradually move towards improvement. You owe it to yourself; keep walking forward, no matter how long it takes.

- Do not anticipate your happiness: Do not feel bad because you feel good! There is no fixed time to recover from your grief. If you find happiness faster, do not feel guilty for not having mourned for too long. If you feel that you have recovered from your loss, it probably means that you have recovered. Do not put a deadline to your sorrow, and do not postpone your happiness either. Never force yourself to be sadder than you are.

Finally

- If someone tells you to move on, do not argue with that person: You will feel worse because you will feel like you have a lower tolerance for emotions than others. In other words, you will begin to believe that there is a problem with the way you handle your grief when there is none. It's just what you feel. Do not listen to them because they do not know the kind of relationship you had with the person you lost. You will heal in your own way after taking the time you need.

- Do not regret anything: Do not demoralize

just because you did not get the opportunity to say I love you or goodbye. You can always say it.

- Remember that everyone feels things differently: Do not worry if you think you're having a harder time getting yourself out of it than someone else — even if you've suffered the same loss. In general, it shows that you and the person you lost had a stronger relationship. Some people will not cry, while others will not be able to stop crying for months.

- You have the right to think of something else: No rule forces you to rehash your loss to prove your sadness or show others that this loss means a lot to you. The others already know that you are devastated; you have nothing to prove or explain.

- Patience is the key: Do not put pressure on yourself as it will heal naturally.

- Music can be a great way to overcome your sense of loss and pain: However, try to choose happy songs, or you may feel sadder by listening to sad music for too long.

- Do not feel guilty: Blaming yourself does

not help, and you will not feel better.

- Life is beautiful; it has many wonderful surprises: Go ahead and smile, visit new places and meet new people.

- Grief works in unique cycles that can vary from person to person: Nobody heals right away, and no one will be extremely angry either.

- If you fall (and you will fall), laugh, kick your buttocks, and keep going!

- Do not be overwhelmed by "and if": For example, "and if I had been nicer." "And if I had taken the time more often to go see him."

- Cry if you need to: Express your emotions. It is not healthy to keep them indoors.

- Try to play with your pets: They know when you are sad, and it might be useful to play with them.

- Do not be afraid to regret certain things because you will regret them, and you will not be able to stop these thoughts, but do not let them direct you. Even if it's difficult to say "I love you" or "I'm sorry" to a person who is present and someone who is gone, try to say it until you believe that person has heard you unless the guilt will always be there. Try to shout what you want to say as loud as you can in an isolated place.

Chapter 7

How Meditation Can Help You

Through the practice of meditation techniques, you can raise your level of peace and prosperity by establishing a relationship of kindness and understanding toward yourself. You learn to be your best friend, and this level of friendship also produces a calming effect on your mood.

As a means of mindfulness, mindfulness is

healthy while suffering mental recreation shows a fact that has caused you pain. Through this introspection, you can internalize and assimilate the information to better understand that pain. This process of acceptance is vital to channel the pain of the wound. You contribute to your own suffering through this attitude of circular thinking around this traumatic event. On the contrary, through mindfulness, you can pause the discursive thought to concentrate your attention on the power of now. And this moment is your main refuge of existential prosperity.

That is, through this practice, you will discover that — at the present moment, there are no emotional ghosts that torment you. Nevertheless, a state of serenity, peace, prosperity, calm, and optimism can be reached through the control of the breath and the power of your mind. Through this self-knowledge process, you will discover that you bring suffering to the present when you update a fact from the past, thereby obsessing your present self with something that no longer exists. That event is only in your mind. The same happens when you worry about the future and fear that something might happen while still in the present.

Through the practice of meditation and positive psychology, you will discover that, as a human being, you have powers marked by existential wisdom. This means you create your reality through your reason, intelligence, sensitivity, intuition, attitude, and will. Therefore, you have the power to overcome those adverse circumstances that make you suffer just by becoming aware of the fact that life gives you new opportunities every day for happiness.

Through meditation, you will also learn that the simplest details of life are the most important. That is, the daily routine gives you a wide range of emotional goods that are your main legacy of well-being. And only through the practice of living in the present can you enjoy these nuances.

Imagine that suffering is like a stone you carry on your shoulders. A heavy load that you one day decide to throw into the sea; only then can you watch the waves take you away. This example can help you understand what I am saying. Through a metaphor, it means to say goodbye to suffering. Through meditation, you learn to acknowledge the power of the present; and open the door of joy, hope, peace, and prosperity.

It is not about turning your back on your pain; it is a human experience that allows you to grow as a person. However, through meditation and positive psychology, you can set your priorities to avoid suffering for what is beyond your control.

Moreover, you learn to deal with your affairs instead of worrying ahead of time about something that transcends your will. This point is important as it is a source of chronic frustration; you pretend to change reality when you cannot.

However, you can change your interior, and from the transformation of this emotional world, your happiness increases. That is — thanks to meditation, mindfulness, and positive psychology, which put light to that pain. Meditation can allow you to stop and experience the first-hand benefits of living a peaceful and prosperous life. This is what the "Create Health Method" is about; it will help you establish new habits in your daily life, not only that you start to meditate, but also to learn how to properly nourish yourself and lead an active life

Chapter 8

Think Healthy, Be Healthy

For more than 40 years, scientists have studied the mind-body connection and the impacts thoughts have on health. Although there is no definitive proof of the exact mechanisms, there is a clear evidence to suggest a clear relationship between mental health and physical health. The simple conclusion is: the easiest way to be healthy is to think healthy thoughts.

Every thought has an immediate impact on biochemistry. The best example of this is stress, where a physical or social threat triggers the "fight or flight" response. This "protection" response floods the body with adrenaline, which increases heartbeat and respiration, but depresses the immune system and other vital functions. Chronic stress is a serious national health problem and more than 80% of all patients visits the doctor. Thinking positive thoughts has the opposite effect; it allows the body enter a profound state of physical and mental relaxation. It's the safety response that leads the body towards optimal function, rejuvenation and repair.

It's easy to understand the benefit of the response to physical threats. After all, you need to quickly respond when a tiger attacks. Yet, thoughts that challenge our idea of who we are or our social standing triggers the same protection response. The only difference is that the threat is being created by the thought of expectation of what might happen.

Worries are stress thoughts in disguise. Chronic worry causes the body to stay in protection mode which depresses the immune and endocrine systems. Over time, the shift is biochemistry and becomes the new "normal" resulting in a chronically-stressed body. The result is a mind-body stress cycle where worried thoughts create a stressed-out body, and the stressed-out body helps create worried thoughts.

Chronic stress depresses the ability to heal and eventually results in dysfunction in one or more critical areas. Long-term dysfunction may lead to further physical degeneration as well as symptom progression before permanent damage. For example; the occasional nervous stomach caused by chronic stress may increase in frequency and severity until it becomes a case of Irritable Bowel Syndrome. Possibility holds that many chronic illnesses like Irritable Bowel Syndrome, Chronic Fatigue Syndrome and Fibromyalgia are the direct result of the mind-body stress cycle.

So, how do you break the cycle? The best way is to stop it before it starts, but that's often easier said than done. Usually, we don't know there's a problem until symptoms appear. When they do, the first step is to reduce the impact of stress on your body. Meditation, yoga and self-hypnosis are great ways to alleviate stress. Unlike meditation and yoga, you can learn self-hypnosis in as little as 30 minutes. And with a little practice, you can reach a deep level of physical, mental and emotional relaxation in 10 minutes or less. De-stressing the body in this way weakens the stress cycle and enables biochemistry to keep moving towards its normal healthy function.

The next step is to change the thought patterns causing stress. Without a doubt, the fastest way to do this is by hypnotherapy. With the guidance of a skilled hypnotherapist, most people change their stressful thought patterns in just a few sessions. Not only does it clear stress triggers but when used with positive affirmations, leads to healthier thought patterns which further supports health.

Self-hypnosis and hypnotherapy break the mind-body stress cycle. When combined with the treatment of your medical professionals, they do not only reduce stress impact on the body but also help you change the thoughts that cause stress. These are two of the best tools you can use to change the way you live your life. Hypnosis and hypnotherapy help you think healthy and be healthy.

The Power of a Healthy Thought

Health is the union of:

- Physical

- Physiological

- Mental

One of the prime laws of Natural Health is the law of Unity — Everything is related and co-related and nothing exists in isolation. Therefore, we do not treat symptoms nor do we look at only parts of the body, rather we treat the entire organism as a whole.

Today, I was the recipient of a lovely email reminding me of the importance of the mind in the role of healing. As we think, so we become.

A mind focused on thoughts of negativity will eventually become diseased.

Some of the more common negative thoughts include:

- Pessimism
- Anger
- Despair
- Failure
- Hatred
- Guilt
- Ignorance
- Violence

The above mentioned thoughts as well as many

others like them will obscure the pathway to health. I remember a 'Charlie Brown' cartoon many years ago, it pictured:

Charlie in a stance of depression — head down, arms hanging limply at his sides and a look of absolute dejection on his face.

Lucy walked up to Charlie and asked why he had assumed this particular posture. Charlie responded that the posture helped him reinforce his feelings.

It is true. We tend to act out our thoughts (consciously or sub-consciously); we become that which we think and say. In the pursuit of high-level health, I recommend the daily practice of repeating positive affirmations.

I used to practise this technique quite religiously, but unfortunately, over the years, I seem to have forgotten the rewards that I reaped from the habit.

However, today is a new day and I am beginning to re-establish an old habit with a new vigour. I sincerely suggest that you take-on the action of:

- With a pen write on paper, a series of positive affirmations on topics that concern you.

- Write them in present positive tense, For example:i.e; "'Today, I am a non-smoker;, no, I'm not going to smoke again." Put them on a spot where you can see them clearly. e.g; on a mirror.
- Make it an habit to read it and repeat each one at least 10 times a day for a week. At the end of the week begin a new affirmation.
- Keep repeating this process until you notice the subtle changes that occur as a result of "'honing your mental abilities through the power of auto-suggestion."

In order to help you with this process, I am going to send you a series of the old affirmations that I wrote down many years ago. Today, my thoughts are centered on expecting only the best and giving only the best.

All the best in becoming the person that you think you are.

Conclusion

ᘓᢙᐧ

This book has shed light on how you can exchange emotional pain for peace and prosperity. Also, we have learned lots of things that can help us to fully cooperate with pain. However, we need to agree with what life has brought for our relationship to change and transform. The more time you spend on this practice, the stronger and easier it will get, and the better and easier your life will become. I didn't believe at first until things started to happen, and life became easier as things began to go my way. The magic starts to flow and becomes a part of your life; that little voice becomes clearer, and the nudges you feel become undeniable. Learn to follow them intuitively without really thinking about it — that is when your life will manifest into what you have always wanted. Barriers dissolve, and your path will light up so that you can easily see.

About Author

Cheryl T. Long is a multi-talented author. A mother of 4 beautiful children and a medical office manager, she loves writing and sharing her stories with all she comes in contact with. She had one vision in her mind — to give people around her an imaginable outlet.

More Books by the Author

Love Yourself (Breaking the Chains of Self-doubt)

Facing the Fear on being Alone How to Deal with the silent treatment

Toxic People who to deal with Them

Letting go of a toxic relationship

Letting Go and Letting God (Ways to surrender control)

Exchange Emotional Pain for Peace and Prosperity

All book available in print and E-book

Stay in touch

www.deardaughterslovesmom. com